MW01624426

Devotional Cinema

Revised Third Edition

Nathaniel Dorsky

Tuumba Press

Acknowledgements:

Publication of the first, second, and third editions of *Devotional Cinema* by Tuumba Press was made possible with the generous support of Owsley Brown III; the author and publisher thank him.

Original version first published in *The Hidden God: Film and Faith* (edited by Mary Lea Bandy and Antonio Monda).

An Italian translation of the first edition of *Devotional Cinema* is published as *Il dio nascosto* (Milan: Edizione Olivares, 2003).

A French translation of the second, revised edition is published as "Le cinéma et la dévotion" in *Trafic*, no. 52, hiver 2004 (Paris: P.O.L. éditeur).

A Spanish translation, *El cine de la devoción*, based on this third, revised text, was published by Asociación Lumière in 2013, translated by Miguel García and edited by Francisco Algarín Navarro.

ISBN 978-1-931157-12-4

Cover photo from *Variations*, a film by Nathaniel Dorsky.

Tuumba Press books are distributed by:
Small Press Distribution
1341 Seventh Street
Berkeley, California 94710-1403
phone: 510-524-1668 or toll-free 800-869-7553
fax: 510-524-0852
email: orders@spdbooks.org
online: www.spdbooks.org

Note to the Reader

Devotional Cinema was originally presented as the John Sacret Young Lecture on March 30, 2001 at Princeton University as part of their Conference on Religion and Cinema. The talk was followed by a screening of three of my films: *Variations*, *Alaya*, and *Arbor Vitae*.

The themes and ideas explored in this presentation were developed over a period of years when I had the pleasure of serving as a guest lecturer at the University of California, Berkeley, the San Francisco Art Institute, and Stanford University.

The text of the original talk was prepared for publication in editorial partnership with Nick Hoff.

Preface to the Third Edition

Since the publication of the second edition of *Devotional Cinema* in 2005, I had the opportunity to teach a semester-long seminar at Princeton University entitled "The Character of Space / Space as Character." In examining closely Carl Theodor Dreyer's *The Passion of Joan of Arc* in this seminar, aspects of it became visible to me for the first time. I also used this opportunity to clarify a number of small points in other sections of the book. The publisher and I agreed that these additions and changes warranted a revised edition.

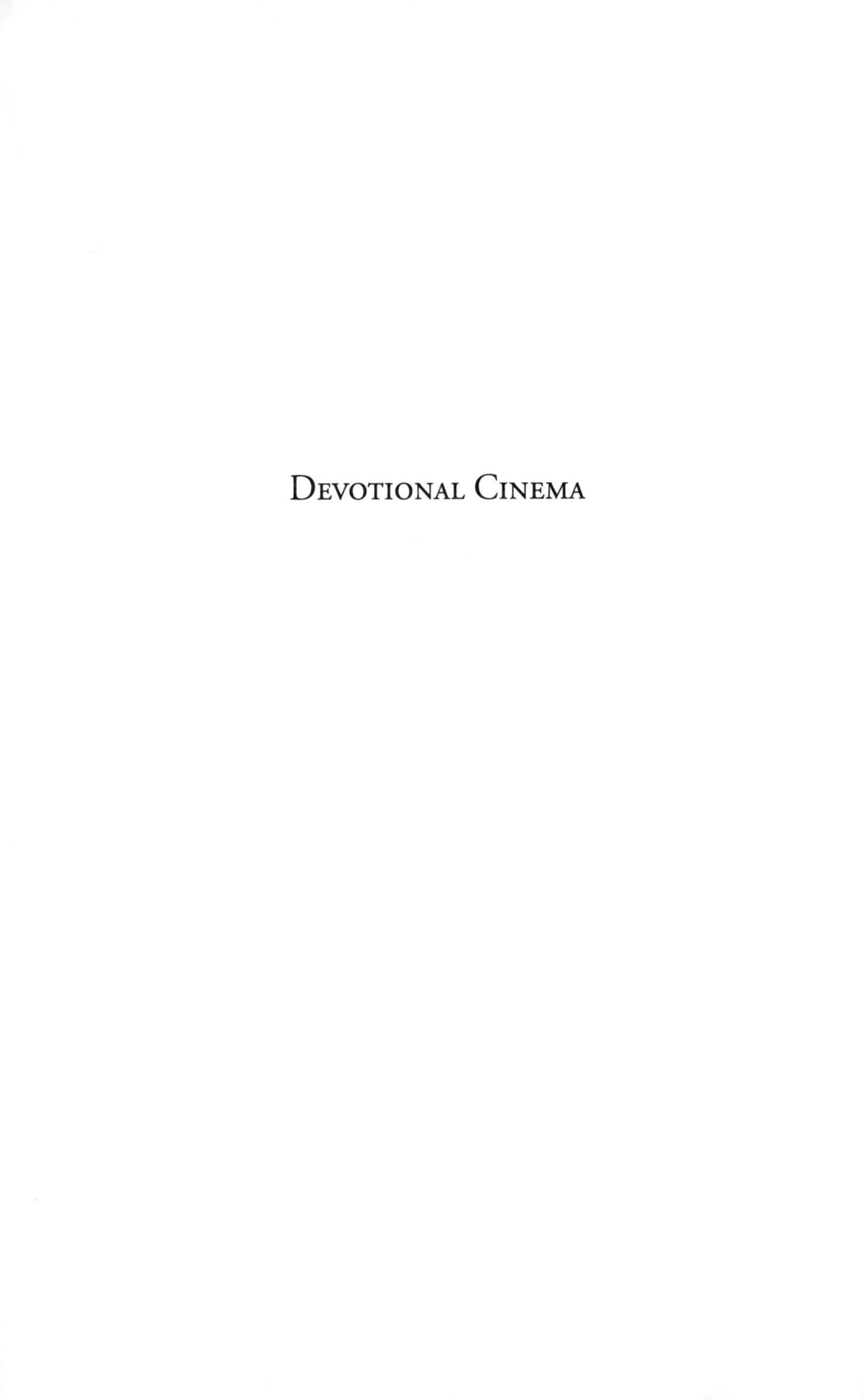

Devotional Cinema

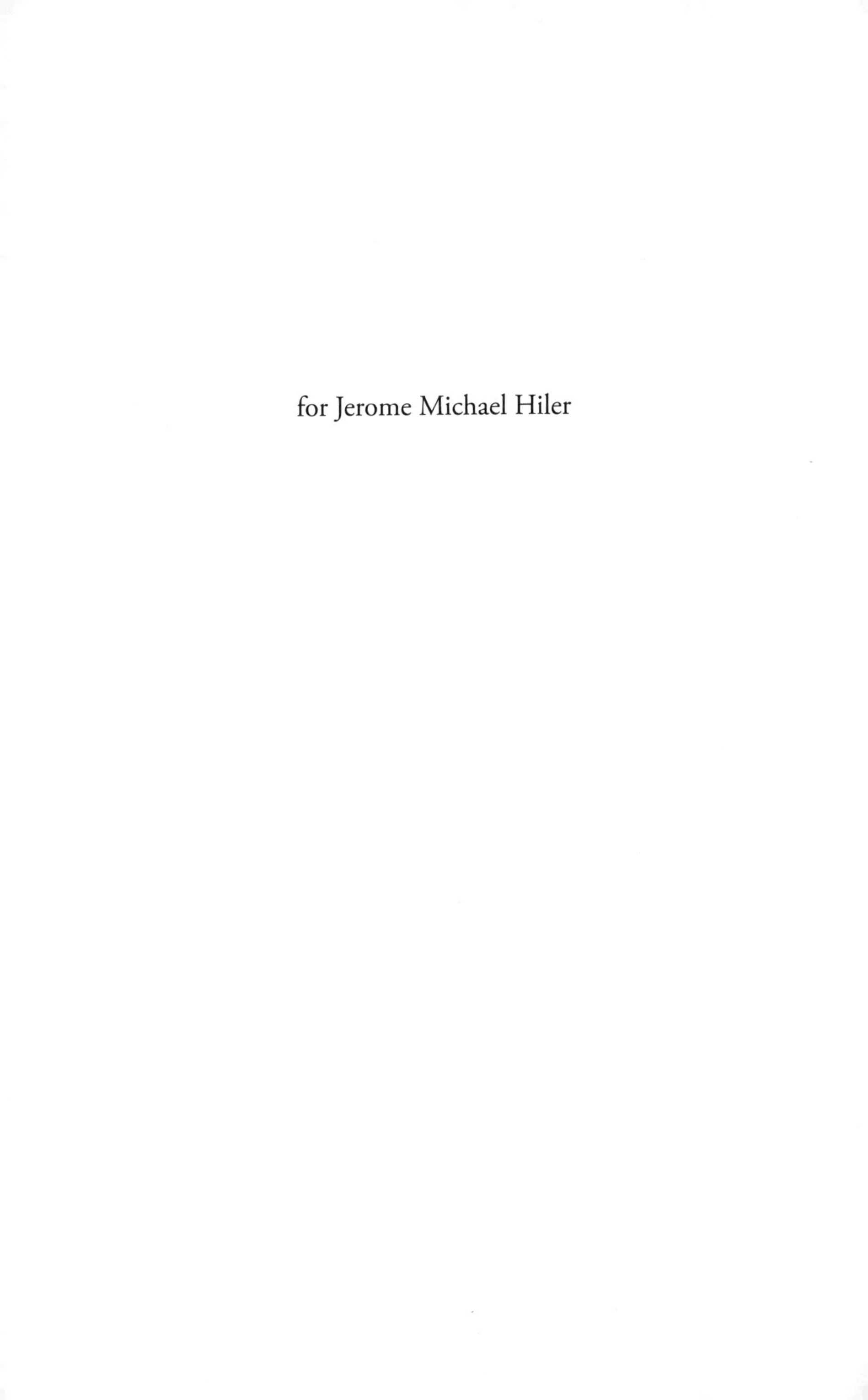

for Jerome Michael Hiler

He did not seem to hear me. But a few moments later he put his hand on mine and his eyes clearly indicated that I should lean closer. He then said very slowly and distinctly the following words, which I record here exactly:

"What does it matter? All is grace."

He died, I believe, just after.

—Georges Bernanos
Diary of a Country Priest

It is a privilege to have been invited to speak on religion and cinema, and I would like to take advantage of this opportunity and speak openly from my heart. Specifically, I would like to talk about devotion and how it might manifest as cinema. I'll reference a small number of feature films, all in the well-known canon, but I would like to be clear at the outset that many other films deserve mention as illustrations of what I'll be discussing.

The relationship between religion and cinema is something that I have spent my life thinking about—not where religion is necessarily the subject of a film, but where film itself is the spirit or experience of religion.

When I first encountered avant-garde films in the early 1960s, the works I found most interesting were those that were discovering a language unique to film, a language that enabled the viewer to have the experience of film itself and, at the same time, allowed film to be an evocation of something meaningfully human. I began to notice that moments of revelation or aliveness came to me from the way a filmmaker used film itself. Shifts of light from shot to shot, for instance, could be very visceral and affective. I observed that there was a concordance between film and our human metabolism, and that this concordance was a fertile ground for expression, a basis for exploring a language intrinsic to film. In fact, film's physical properties seemed so attuned to our metabolism that I began to experience film as a direct and intimate metaphor or model for our being, a model which had the potential to be transformative, to be an evocation of spirit, and to become a form of devotion.

The word "devotion," as I am using it, need not refer to the embodiment of a specific religious form. Rather, it is the opening or the interruption that allows us to experience what is hidden, and to accept with our hearts our given situation. When film does this, when it subverts our absorption in the temporal and reveals the depths of our own reality, it opens us to a fuller sense of ourselves and our world. It is alive as a devotional form.

The Formal Situation

As human beings we find ourselves in a strange situation. We have the same basic qualities, problems, emotions, and interests that animals have: we experience danger and often need to defend ourselves, we need to eat and sleep, we feel anger and tenderness, and we reproduce. At the same time we also have the ability to observe this entire experience, to see through the moments of anger, fear, and tenderness rather than just experience them. We are part of our experience and yet we can see through it. We can see through it, yet we are not free from it. We are both appreciators and victims of material existence.

Human beings are born, live for a certain period of time, and die. There's no denying that form. After all, here we are, on a planet, illuminated by a glowing star. There's air and light, in which we all participate. The ocean rises and falls with the moon. The temperature is at least reasonable, and we have the freedom to walk around and look at things. At times we feel alone; we desire, we fall in love. We might think that all this is our own discovery, that we are actually responsible for all this. Yet we didn't make up any of these possibilities. Even the fact that we have ideas or values, or clarity or confusion for that matter—none of this is our creation. We did not make up our emotions. We did not make up the fact that we find things beautiful or that people fall in love. After all, I don't even know how I move my hand or turn my head. I don't even know how I'm speaking. All I know is that I can participate in this situation.

At first this realization might seem disconcerting. We might try to escape or distract ourselves. But the more we are able to relax and accept the absolute presence of our situation and then begin to recognize its formal qualities, the greater the chance we have to transmute it. With humility we can perform an act of alchemy and transform what might feel like leaden claustrophobia into an expression of openness and clarity. But how can cinema be an act of alchemy? How can it elucidate the formality of our being and participate in devotion?

The Post-film Experience

I think the first time I began to suspect that film was powerful, even something to be feared, was when I was nine years old. This was in the early 1950s, before television had become all-pervasive. I used to go to the movies on Saturday afternoons, and on one particular day there was a special kiddie matinee that included three features, ten cartoons, and a good dose of previews, all in one sitting. We entered into darkness at twelve noon and came out hours later at 6:30. As the last film ended, the green metal side doors opened into the late-afternoon light, and we walked up the alley onto the street. I remember having the oddest sensation. The texture of the sunlight seemed strange, and people's voices sounded distant. In front of the theater cars were whooshing by the storefronts. Quite suddenly, the normal things that were my usual reference points, everything that had been familiar to me in my hometown, all its archetypes and icons, became eerie and questionable. I felt alien and estranged. I remember walking home alone through the park and passing the duck pond and the baseball diamonds, and then down a small path, a dirt shortcut worn through the lawn that eventually disappeared into the grass. All those little details were presenting themselves to me in a way I was unused to. It was truly disturbing. Eventually I got home, and it even seemed odd that I was in my house. I was feeling this quite strongly and was trying my best to recover from the giant hole that had opened up in the middle of my head. I remember having to get some things out of the refrigerator to reorient myself and make it all right again.

In my twenties I had an equally significant experience after seeing Roberto Rossellini's *Voyage to Italy* at the old Museum of Modern Art in San Francisco. Many filmmakers and critics feel that modern cinema began with this movie. Made in 1953, it is a work that changed film history, but it is also relatively unknown.

Voyage to Italy involves an English couple, played by George Sanders and Ingrid Bergman, who travel by car to Naples in order to sell a house they have inherited. While in Naples, they find themselves alone together, really for the first time in their marriage. All their business and household concerns have been left behind. They begin to argue in the first scene of the movie; in fact the movie is an hour-and-a-half-long argument. It is a real love story—*the* great love story.

Like all of Rossellini's work, *Voyage to Italy* searches for authenticity with unguarded nakedness. These two people are stuck, each in their own view of life and their view of each other. The very timbre of their voices is dismantling and heartbreaking. They snap at one another to the point of absolute impasse, until there's no way out except through divorce or renunciation.

The quality of the filmmaking is primitive yet graceful, extremely intelligent but without vanity or polish. The montage is buoyant and extremely practical. It has the same rawness and sense of exploration and discovery that the couple is experiencing. *Voyage to Italy* is not a film about a subject, rather it is the subject. It is so direct and effective that one cannot say exactly why it functions with so much power. The actual fabric of Rossellini's film, the rightness and invisibility of its form, is deeply disarming. The state of vulnerability it produces in the audience, this heartbreak, this not-knowing, is the catalyst that brings forth our renunciation and connects us to devotion.

After the film, the audience entered the elevator in order to descend to the street, and I noticed that everybody was unusually available to everybody else. People had tears in their eyes. Usually the time in an elevator is a "no" time. We either stare up at the numbers or down at the floor, trying to deny the intimacy of the situation. We wait for this "no" time to be over so that we can resume our lives. But in this case everyone was completely accessible and vulnerable to one another, looking at each other, all strangers within the intimate compartment of an elevator.

I began to wonder about what this post-film experience is. How do we feel when a film is over? There are films, for instance, that are intellectually rigorous, or "adult," but when the lights come up at the end of them we feel unhealthy in some way. We're embarrassed to be with one another. We've all had the experience of walking out of a theater and not really wanting to see anyone—of looking down at the bizarre design on the rug, the soda stains, and so forth, and averting our eyes from our fellow filmgoers. I realized from these experiences that there was something in cinema beyond its intellectual or narrative content. There was something in the actual nature of cinema, its view, that could produce health or illness in an audience. There might be a film that had a very meaningful subject but was so inelegantly handled that it actually left one feeling unhealthy or alienated.

I began to become more sensitive to these post-film experiences and the qualities in a film that might produce either health or ill health. I knew from my experience that this possibility extended into other media. I remember once being quite sick when my friend Jerome and I went to a student production of

Così fan tutte at a local college. I didn't want to go but I went anyway. And when I came out of the opera, I was completely cured. The youthful performance was endearing and sometimes painful, but because the genius of the music is so uncompromised, so transforming to the metabolism, the experience of going to the opera healed me. This has happened to me quite a few times from going to a Mozart opera.

Similarly, attending the ballets of George Balanchine can realign one's energy in a way that is deeply, alchemically healthy. I believe this occurs when there is something metaphysically true about a work's energy. In Greek theories of medicine it was taught that illness came from a dreamlike absorption, a state of imbalance. The sanctuary of Epidaurus was created in order to let citizens realign themselves and awaken to the full energy of the present. Long periods of relaxation and sleep, called "temple sleep," were followed by theater pieces, chanting, and poetry. All this took place in a setting of sublimely proportioned architecture. So art has had a long history of being used as a healthy model.

What is it about the nature of film that can produce health or ill health? It is film's ability to mirror and realign our metabolism.

Alchemy

For alchemy to take place in a film, the form must include the expression of its own materiality, and this materiality must be in union with its subject matter. If this union is not present, if the film's literalness is so overwhelming, so illustrative, that it obliterates the medium it is composed of, then one is seduced into a dream state of belief or absorption that, though effective on that level, lacks the necessary ingredients for transmutation. Such a film denies its totality. It denies the fact of what it is actually made of.

The instinct to express the union of material and subject occurs at the beginning of known human expression. The devotional cave art in southern France and northern Spain often plays with the contours of the cave walls to enhance the hallucination of the bison or horse depicted on them. Egyptian sculpture is as much about the unceasing nature of stone as it is about the unceasing glance engraved on that stone. In French religious stone carving of the late twelfth century, the stone itself is luminous, as both material and expression. The stained glass of the same period was born out of a love of the elemental glory of light, color, and glass, while at the same time relating biblical tales or the lives of saints. Similarly, Bach's organ chorale preludes are as much an expression of skeletal fingers pressing down on ivory keys and releasing air through pipes as they are melodic evocations of prayer. Mozart, born into the age of classicism, wedded his classical style to the human metabolism in every detail. The texture of the instrumentation, the key changes, and the depiction of conversation and emotion through melodic line are the music itself and at the same time are a primordial mirror or example of what it is to be fully human. We hear ourselves at our alchemical best.

For film to partake in this luminosity and elemental glory, and thereby lay the ground for devotion, it must obey its own materiality. Let's examine the nature of that materiality and how it is a metaphor for our being.

The Illuminated Room

We view films in the context of darkness. We sit in darkness and watch an illuminated world, the world of the screen. This situation is a metaphor for the nature of our own vision. In the very process of seeing, our own skull is like a dark theater, and the world we see in front of us is in a sense a screen. We watch the world from the dark theater of our skull. The darker the room, the more luminous the screen.

It is important to understand what we're participating in, to realize that we rest in darkness and experience vision. Many people take vision as a given and don't realize that they are actually seeing.

Throughout history, there have been many different ideas about where vision takes place. The art of various eras seems to indicate this. In the Middle Ages there was a sense that the source of illumination wasn't necessarily outside ourselves but that we were perhaps the source of that light, that our human experience might be compared to a luminous bubble suspended in darkness. Stained glass windows of that period were an expression of this, an echo of our self-luminosity. The cathedrals were dark, vast caverns with stained glass windows forming the surface of a world, a world of suspended illumination. There was no external world as such. After spending an extended period of time in the Cathedral of Notre-Dame at Chartres, for instance, one begins to see the world in that way. Upon exiting the cathedral we find ourselves attuned to this view, and see the visual world as self-luminous and resting on a profound vastness, the mysterious darkness of our own being.

During the Renaissance this idea of vision shifted and we began to understand the world as something more objectively outside ourselves. Cathedral windows became progressively more clear; the internal vastness vanished from the psyche and we began to understand the seen world as an objectively observed world, a total world. It is quite a change. We peer out toward a vanishing point. There is a new sense of science.

Where does vision take place? It is an age-old question. Is everything mind or is everything not mind? It is interesting to think that everything we see might be only an aspect of the mind. Sometimes I actually experience this: turning my head to look around, I realize that what I'm seeing is just an image field shifting, an aspect of my own brain. But then I can experience the opposite and say no, the world is really out there and I'm here looking at it. It's really there and is not dependent on my seeing it.

But beyond these two extremes is our normal daily experience. We simply see. We cannot describe it but only experience it. Film, insofar as it replicates our experience of vision, presents us with the tools to touch on and elucidate that experience. Viewing a film has tremendous mystical implications; it can be, at its best, a way of approaching and manifesting the ineffable. This respect for the ineffable is an essential aspect of devotion.

When cinema can make the internalized medieval and externalized Renaissance ways of seeing unite and transcend themselves, it can achieve a transcendental balance. This balance point unveils the transparency of our earthly experience. We are afloat. It is a balance that is neither our vision nor the belief in exterior objectivity; it belongs to no one and, strangely enough, exists nowhere. It is within this balance that the potential for profound cinema takes place.

Less visionary cinema is imbalanced toward one or the other of these two ways of seeing. One imbalance assumes that the world is out there and you are going to photograph it. In this case there is no view whatsoever; the subject matter seems somehow just to exist. That the film is even a film is somewhat arbitrary. We see these movies every time we get on an airplane, or wander desperately into our local multiplex. This form of film ignores the very substance it is made of. There is certainly no awareness of the formal dignity of existence that we have been speaking about.

The other imbalance occurs when there is nothing *but* the view of the filmmaker, when nothing in the film is really permitted to exist in its own right. This single-mindedness eliminates the possibility of any autonomy within the film; the film has no ability to respond or resonate within itself. The filmmaker's vanity dominates and controls. There is no freedom, no air to breathe. How often we experience this at a first-run art house or avant-garde venue.

These imbalances distort what life actually could be for humans. They are an inversion of the hierarchy of vision, language, and concept, a hierarchy that, if balanced properly, can sublimely inform our daily experience. That is, first we are in visual space, and then, within that three-dimensional context, we speak and declare. This space allows us to both see and feel the world more clearly—our heart softens and opens and our intuition is in place.

Films have the potential to mirror this clarity, but all too often represent spoken-language ideas rather than recognizing that concepts or spoken language are ornaments in the context of visual space. The ornament of language can point out, direct, specify, and describe the world, but it doesn't see the world. Many films suffer from this distortion. Sometimes it is quite obvious. For instance, the syntax of the television-style documentary film, like that of the evening news, often turns the visual vitality of the world into mere wallpaper in support of spoken information. I think if Dante were writing the *Inferno* today, the first ring of Hell would be a large circular desk of newscasters.

There is an extremely subtle but significant difference between an image that is in itself a manifested act of seeing and one that uses vision to represent the world. One partakes in the living present and appreciates the world as something actually seen, while the other is secondary, a muted copy of the world. Many films are delicately subservient to an idea or theme and consequently the images are never allowed to exist as themselves. They illustrate a scripted, written reality or concept. Even if they are visual, they are self-consciously so. They represent another form, a literary one, rather than manifesting directly as vision. This subtle distortion of the vision-language hierarchy violates the primordial strength of what cinema has to offer. It flattens our reality and flattens out cinema. It is a far cry from the primordial ground of the illuminated room and the need for film to respect reality—the reality of being in the dark theater of our skull, observing incandescence.

Intermittence

The quality of light, as experienced in film, is intermittent. At sound speed there are twenty-four images a second, each about a fiftieth of a second in duration, alternating with an equivalent period of black. So the film we are watching is not actually a solid thing. It only appears to be solid.

On a visceral level, the intermittent quality of film is close to the way we experience the world. We don't experience a solid continuum of existence. Sometimes we are here and sometimes not, suspended in some kind of rapid-fire illusion. After all, do any of us know *who* we actually are? Although we assume that we are something solid, in truth we only experience and maneuver through our existence. After all, can anything really be solid?

On close examination, even our vision appears to be intermittent, which explains why, in film, pans often feel artificial or forced. This stems from the fact that one never pans in real life. In truth, when we turn our heads we don't actually see a graceful continuum but a series of tiny jump-cuts, little stills joined, perhaps, by infinitesimal dissolves. Thus our visual experience in daily life is akin to the intermittence of cinema.

Intermittence penetrates to the very core of our being, and film vibrates in a way that is close to this core. It is as basic as life and death, existence and nonexistence. My own instinct is that the poles of existence and nonexistence alternate at an extremely fast speed, and that we float in that alternation. We don't experience the nonexistence, the moments between existence; there is no way to perceive these moments as such. But accepting their presence aerates life, and suffuses the "solid" world with luminosity.

A second aspect of intermittence has to do with the nature of montage, the play of events or the narrative nature of our lives. This intermittence is part of our daily experience. For example, you might be driving your car and your mind wanders off into thought, two red lights, and a left turn later you return to your driving and think, "Who was driving? How did I do that? I stopped at red lights. Where was I?" In other words, life is full of gaps. We try to make the whole thing seem continuous and solid, but it's actually more intermittent than we often want to admit. In a sense, for film to be true, it has to trust this intermittence. Its montage has to present a succession of visual events that are sparing enough, and at the same time poignant enough, to allow the viewer's most basic sense of existence to "fill in the blanks." If a film fills in too much, it violates our experience.

We certainly know the shallow, sickening feeling of leaving a film that has had no true respect for the intermittence of our being. Such a film does not respect what we know life to be, it is not what we experience. It is too solid. It is an act of rudeness.

Allowing intermittence into a film activates the viewer's mind. There is an opportunity to make connections, to feel alive and stimulated. Making these connections, activating these synapses, brings the viewer into the present moment.

Time

A third important aspect of film's materiality comes from its need to express itself in time. Time is one of the essential elements in film's alchemy. It is one of the most potent tools film has, yet few films connect profoundly with the plasticity of time and use the nature of time in their structure. It is the substance that, when handled properly, opens the door to the possibility of devotion.

There are two basic types of time in filmmaking. The first could be called relative time, which is how any film progresses from the first shot to the last. How a river flows from a mountain to the ocean, or how we progress from crawling infants to old people with walkers. The qualities of relative time are both subtle and dramatic: every river has white water followed by deep, translucent pools, then swirling currents, stagnant backwaters with mosquitoes, places where foam and sludge pile up. There are spectacular, frothy waterfalls and flat little rippling areas glistening in sunlight. A complete emotional range exists in our experience of relative time, and a film must respect these qualities. They are part of our lives.

At the same time, inspired filmmaking includes the presence of the other type of time: what might be called absolute time, or nowness. Nowness is always . . . nowness. Every moment of time exists in the context of nowness, the eternal now. Experiencing the relationship of nowness to relative time is akin to walking on a treadmill: the nowness is your presence while relative time passes under your feet. Nowness in cinema deeply respects the nowness in an audience.

If one looks at an Egyptian votive sculpture from 4,000 years ago, one can appreciate its uncompromising presence. The Egyptian sculptor's direct experience of nowness is being communicated in the present moment. Being able to experience nowness and experiencing it in a work of art allows you to participate directly with the very heart of that work and its maker. You are right there with them, sharing their vision. There is a secret underground of continual transmission that is possible within human society and relative time, sitting magically right in front of us but often not seen. It occurs through someone's inspiration to put something into the world that is uncompromisingly present, which, in turn, invokes our innate ability to share in that presence.

In all the various moods and styles through which relative time has manifested, great artists have always expressed nowness. Standing behind the Cathedral of Notre Dame in Paris and contemplating its grace and geometry, the delicate traceries of its rose windows, and the functional integrity of its buttresses and spires, one experiences the timeless splendor of pure nowness. Pure nowness transcends the passage of time.

For film to have a devotional quality both absolute and relative time must be active and present—

not only present but functioning simultaneously and invigorating one another. Transformative film rests in the present and respects the delicate details of its own unfolding. How is this small miracle achieved? How do we manifest nowness in the ongoing context of the relative? It is not unlike having a heartfelt discussion with a friend. You hear what your friend says, and you respond from a place you may never have responded from before. You hear your friend again, you wait a second, and there's an actual moment of connection, a moment of genuine exploration that touches upon things never quite touched on before. That's when heart, intelligence, instinct, and awareness all come together. Reality opens and responds to itself.

We are certainly all familiar with moments that are not like this. Conversation can often be an exhausting exchange of self-confirming, predigested concepts with no real exploration: everything is already "known" and is motivated by a need to maintain the status quo of oneself in relation to the other person. Nowness is tainted by the need to accomplish something, to stay in control.

Film has this same potential to be balanced or imbalanced. For instance, if a film is excessively horizontal, excessively temporal, it may succeed in being seductive and absorbing, but it may also leave one feeling shallow and used. It evades the totality of our awareness. A film can also be imbalanced in the other extreme. In this case its verticality or nowness is reified to the point that the film ignores the demands and nuances of the temporal, or is so absorbed in its own profundity that it numbs the mind of the viewer.

Integrating these two qualities of time is a difficult and delicate task. Carl Theodor Dreyer accomplishes this in *The Passion of Joan of Arc* (1928) and *Ordet* (1955), films made in different periods of his career. *The Passion of Joan* is silent and visually enlivened by dramatic close-ups, confrontational cuts, and bold, angular camera movements. Each shot, while participating in the progression of the narrative's temporality is also an evocation of pure vertical nowness. Each shot is both of and in itself a character. Each has its own particular sense of space. The cuts that bring together these various elements are often propelled by the characters' head movements and facial gestures. The film is an inspired union of form and subject. All is present.

Dreyer accomplishes this feat of cinematic magic in a most involving way. Time and time again, we, the audience, see the judges' aggression unfold from Joan's point of view, which becomes our own point of view. We experience their abuse as something delivered directly to us. We become Joan. But when Dreyer cuts to Joan, it is not from a neutral storytelling point of view, nor is it from the judges' syntactically correct point of view, which would be looking down at her, but it is a view that is a pure and loving, ever so slightly upward angle that embraces her in adoration. Again and again, we the audience directly receive the abuse coming down from the tribunal, and only after experiencing that pain directly do we cut to see the aftermath, the suffering grace of Joan, her face longing for heaven. We have become through the montage the very conduit between these opposing worlds. We have become active participants in the film's spatial unfolding. Our identification with Joan is thorough, compassionate, and ever-present. We experience her as an unflinching manifestation of nowness within the relative time of the narrative.

Ordet, made some thirty years later, has sound and a bare minimum of close-ups and character-motivated intercuts, which are reserved for the concluding scene.* The strange altered light in this film, both interior and exterior, sets us in a suspended time. We are privileged to participate in a rare and purified world, a world of transformation. Time and space are never collapsed by temporal necessity. We find ourselves immersed in the long, flowing, earthbound takes. The ongoingness of

*P. Adams Sitney speaks so well of this in his book *Modernist Montage: The Obscurity of Vision in Cinema and Literature* (New York: Columbia University Press, 1990).

the shots allows us to deepen our experience of nowness. Gaps in the narrative open up within the continuum of the shots. As the camera follows a character from one section of the room to another, the dialogue and character placement intensify and decompress, along with the energy of the drama. Between these moments of intensity we are lulled into relaxation, and thus when the shot intensifies again we feel our presence all the more strongly. This intensification sometimes happens through the unexpected entrance of a character into the frame, sometimes by a cut to the next unfolding event. This continual renewal gives the mystical intensity of the climactic scene a living presence, a grounded reality.

Both films successfully balance the nowness and temporal aspects of time while completely integrating them with the text and the revelation of character and story. But a film like *Day of Wrath*, which Dreyer made twelve years before *Ordet*, seems to sacrifice the pure existence of nowness. Although the first shot foreshadows the sublime syntax of *Ordet*, *Day of Wrath* seems to violate the sense of time that the shot establishes. The camera placement soon becomes awkward and the relative and absolute aspects of the film seem at war with each other. The depth and sincerity of the photography is not supported by the D. W. Griffith-like syntax of the plot- and dialogue-motivated cutting. The film seems torn between an instinctive allegiance to nowness and the needs of the scripted story. The absolute and direct quality of the images is sacrificed. The temporal does not complement the nowness but punctures it. Everything is done very well, of course, but no unguarded sense of the present is allowed to manifest for the viewer. In a subtle way, the images are not alive, they do not reveal themselves as the present. The sequences *illustrate* something rather than *are* something in themselves.

When the absolute and temporal are unified, film becomes a narrative of nowness and reveals things for what they are rather than as surrogates for some predetermined concept. It is the fear of direct contact with the uncontrollable present that motivates the flight into concept. The filmmaker seeks the safety net of an idea, or something to accomplish that is already known.

If we do relinquish control, we suddenly see a hidden world, one that has existed all along right in front of us. In a flash, the uncanny presence of this poetic and vibrant world, ripe with mystery, stands before us. Everything is expressing itself as what it is. Everything is alive and talking to us.

Self-Symbol

If you have ever looked at your hand and seen it freshly without concept, realized the simultaneity of its beauty, its efficiency, its detail, you are awed into appreciation. The total genius of your hand is more profound than anything you could have calculated with your intellect. One's hand is a devotional object.

If a film fails to take advantage of the self-existing magic of things, if it uses objects merely to mean something, it has thrown away one of its great possibilities. When we take an object and make it mean something, what we are doing, in a subtle or not so subtle way, is confirming ourselves. We are confirming our own concepts of who we are and what the world is. But allowing things to be seen for what they are offers a more open, more fertile ground than the realm of predetermined symbolic meaning. After all, the unknown is pure adventure.

Yasujiro Ozu is of course a great exponent of self-symbol. Every shot, every cut, every character, every situation of the story, while definitely functioning in the context of a narrative, is not referring to anything but itself. Each moment opens in terms of what it actually is.

There is an interesting lesson of self-symbol in Ozu's first sound film, *The Only Son* (1936). It is a story about a poor single mother and her young son. The boy wants to go to the expensive private school that his friends are planning to attend. He cries and cries and finally his mother relents. We see her working long hours in a factory over the years to pay the exorbitant fees. Then Ozu takes a leap in time, which is unusual for him, and we meet the son, now in his late twenties, in an unhappy marriage, with a young child, a mediocre teaching job, and living in an industrial suburb of Tokyo. His mother is coming to visit him for the first time since he's left home. Ozu's narratives often concern such primal scenes in our lives, iconic scenes that we all know deeply. These incidents themselves are self-symbols, primal incidents, not just devices to further absorb us in the plot.

When his mother arrives, we feel her disappointment and also the son's embarrassment at what his life has come to. He cannot admit this embarrassment and acts defensively toward her. We feel her sadness and remember her sacrifice. To keep her entertained and to distract her from this painful situation, he takes her to the movies one night. She's a country woman, and she's probably never been to the movies. We sense that it's an uncomfortable thing for her to do, that it's a slightly abrasive situation. But he takes her to a movie and they sit and watch a German film and we see them and the film they are watching.

The camera in the German film, so unlike Ozu's, is constantly in motion. We see dolly shots of a peasant boy and girl as they run through fields of wheat. As they embrace, the girl succumbs, dropping her handkerchief to the ground. We cut to see it lying there. The dropping of the handkerchief is clearly symbolic of her submission and is treated as a literary metaphor.

The uncompromised presence in *The Only Son* is the antithesis of this type of expression. Near the end of the mother's visit, Ozu offers us one of his poignant set pieces. We see the son and his mother settling down on an abandoned hill to talk. Below, not far in the distance, an incinerator billows smoke into the sky. Our characters, in a moment of vulnerability, finally open to one another with unguarded honesty and tenderness. He asks if she is disappointed in him and confesses to his own unhappiness. Perhaps he should never have left her. They sit and talk and we feel the pain and impossibility of their situation. Hearing the sound of a sky lark the son pauses and looks upward. Ozu cuts to a full-frame shot of the sky. We rest in this transparency and then cut to the mother sitting beside her son. Her head is lowered, weighed down by all that has transpired. Then she too raises her gaze and once more we cut to an open shot of the sky. We take in its lightness and then cut again. We see the incinerator, its large stacks spewing forth dark smoke. In a reverse angle, the mother and son walk away across the open field. There is no summation to all these elements, only the direct experience of poetic mystery and the resonance of self-symbol.

This marriage of narrative necessity and self-symbol is also apparent in the films of Michelangelo Antonioni. His modernist Italian temperament gives the screen a very different flavor from that of Ozu, but it also manifests the present as self-symbol. Antonioni had the good fortune to be able to make a number of short films before his first feature. Right from the beginning, his understanding of cinema was apparent. His first feature film, *Story of a Love Affair* (1950), may be one of the greatest first features ever made. He already understood and integrated the plasticity of cinema with the plasticity of the narrative. Every shot is the narrative and the narrative is every shot. This integrity continues throughout the black and white period of his career.

In *La Notte* (1960), for instance, the real beauty of the film, the real depth of its intelligence, continues to lie in the clarity of the montage—the way the world is revealed to us moment by moment. The camera's delicate interactive grace, participating with the fluidity of the characters' changing points of view, is profound in itself. Early in the film, Lidia (Jeanne Moreau) and Giovanni (Marcello Mastroianni) are visiting a dying friend in a hospital room. At one point the sick man's mother enters and sits down on the periphery of the scene, allowing the three friends to continue their conversation. The camera caresses the three characters as they move about the room. We become absorbed in their conversation and then Lidia excuses herself, leaving Giovanni alone with the friend. Suddenly we cut to a shot from behind the mother's head, as she watches the bedside scene. This simple shot is startling. It has no particular symbolic meaning but allows us to see the hospital room and the interrelated presence of the characters unexpectedly from the mother's perspective. We watch from this angle for some time. The moment ripens. We then cut to a very wide exterior of the hospital with Lidia a tiny figure at the lower left, and then to a medium shot with her leaning against the wall on the right. Then a cut to Giovanni on the left, opening the door of the hospital room into the slightly darker hallway, and a nurse walks by preceded by her shadow and enters a door behind him, helping to motivate the camera move down the hallway with our character. The rightness of all these shifts of space, the weight of light and darkness, are the meaning, the aliveness, and the beauty of the film. All is present, all is functioning.

A little later on, though, there's a moment that seems somewhat less realized, where the images are used symbolically to communicate a language-based idea. When the film first came out, this moment seemed very important. It was, after all, begging to be deciphered and explained. Lidia takes a long walk during her husband's book-signing. The direct brilliance of the shots and cuts during this sequence is as fresh today as when it was first made. The very fabric of the screen sparkles with self-symbol. In this walk we see her displaying and testing her attractiveness. Released from her marriage, she wanders through a dreamlike world, a world of male symbols, but the primary expression is the beauty and poetry of the montage. Then at one point she comes upon a half-demolished building and enters the yard. A small child is heard crying and Lidia walks over, attempts to comfort her, then turns and walks away. We cut to a shot that looks down at a broken clock on the ground as Lidia's arm enters the frame. This is followed by a shot of her hand fingering some decayed, rusty metal. This meaning-laden succession of cinematic events, perhaps symbolic of her failing and childless marriage, involves a subtle shift in syntax and removes us from the immediacy of what we've been experiencing. There definitely is meaning, but so much less so than in the existential directness and openness of the cinema that surrounds this moment.

The film, however, easily recovers and rebalances itself. We see Giovanni return to their apartment and lie down to rest, and then, as he flicks the curtain, we cut and rejoin Lidia as this memorable cinematic walk continues. We eventually see a graceful shot of her passing in front of a row of trees as she comes upon a group of young men setting off rockets in a field. She joins a group of observers. As the scene ends, we see a cloud of rocket smoke begin to drift toward her, as seen from her point of view. We cut to a reverse angle of the group and see Lidia turn and walk away from the camera, eventually being framed in the foreground by two of the observers. We wait for the cloud of smoke to envelop the scene. Instead, we cut unexpectedly to Giovanni asleep in his darkened apartment, foregrounded by the blowing pages of an open book and some other papers. The movement of the wind is continued from the smoke shot, but not directly; it is delayed by the shot of Lidia leaving. This produces an intermittent connective for the viewer. There is a continuity of the wind but with a dreamlike replacement of subject matter. With this synapse activated, the film is literally living in the minds of the audience.

How does a film go from mere representation to the type of direct experience we've been talking about? It depends, for one, on the filmmaker's realizing that the screen itself is essential to our experience of a film, that it is its own self-symbol.

Not to respect the screen as its own self-symbol is to treat film as a medium for information. It is to say that the whole absorbing mechanism of projected light—the shots, the cuts, the actors—is there only to represent a scripted idea. But film at its transformative best is not primarily a literary medium. The screen or the field of light on the wall must be alive as sculpture, while at the same time expressing the iconography within the frame. Beyond everything else, film is a screen, film is a rectangle of light, film is light sculpture in time. How does a filmmaker sculpt light in harmony with its subject matter? How can light be deeply in union with evocation? How do you construct a temporal form that continues to express nowness to the audience?

Shots and Cuts

Shots and cuts are the two elemental opposites that enable film to transform itself. Shots are the accommodation, the connection, the empathy, the view of the subject matter we see on the screen. The cuts are the clarity that continually reawakens the view. When there is a balance of these essential elements, a film blossoms as light in the present tense and gives devotion the space to manifest. Shots and cuts must each participate in this clarity.

If the filmmaker is not cognizant of the fact

that a shot must express both the seer and what is seen, then the film's view isn't totally conscious. The view is make-believe; it does not admit that vision is a meeting ground of ourselves and the world. The filmmaker and what is seen are not in union. The basic ingredients for alchemy are not present. So the question becomes: how does a filmmaker selflessly unite the viewer with what is seen? If there is too much self, then there is too much view. This imbalance often manifests as the empty vanity of composition that overwhelms a less-felt subject matter. On the other hand, if there is too much subject matter, then there is no view. This imbalance ignores or sacrifices the visual fabric of film, which is its strongest aspect, and the image becomes too illustrative. In either case the film's vision is one-dimensional. Light in union with subject is no longer an active element.

The camera must give itself completely and wholly to its subject, yet it cannot give itself away to its subject. When a filmmaker is fully and selflessly present, the audience becomes fully and selflessly present. The filmmaker's physical relationship to the world manifests as the camera's relationship to the image and becomes the audience's relationship to the screen. To the degree that a filmmaker can relate directly to the heart of an object, the viewer will also connect directly to the heart of the object. The audience will see the screen as the camera sees the objects, and a great unity of heart will take place between filmmaker and audience.

Shots and cuts need each other. They are cinema's primal handmaidens. The shots, as moments of luminous accommodation, ripen and expand and are popped like soap bubbles by the cut. The cuts redeclare the clarity of the shots, restating the primal clarity of the view. Otherwise the shots become too solid. For cinema to be transformative, there must be a balance between these two basic elements. If a film is cut in a manner that forces the progression of the shots, not allowing the shots to come into fullness, then no connection with presence can take place. In such a film, the aggressive cutting might mask the emptiness of the view. On the other hand, if the poignancy of what a cut has to offer is ignored, or if the shots are so excessively proud and varnished with visual egoism that cutting from them would be a disruption to the visual surface itself, then the delicacy of this essential counterbalance cannot develop. In the former case the film is too armored and evasive, in the latter too self-serious and solid.

Cuts seem to work in a hierarchy. First, a cut has to work on a visual level, in terms of shape, texture, color, movement, and weight. Somehow the shift from one shot to the next has to create a visual freshness for the psyche. Something happens to the nature of the cinematic space that is right. This quality is so intrinsic to film that it is difficult to describe. In a film that we love, each progressing moment enlivens and deepens the subject and our experience of the screen simultaneously.

When the cut works visually, two aftershocks may occur. The first is in the area of dream connectives, or poetry—the way our mind uses images in its own nighttime arena. The sudden shift in space caused by the cut enlivens the unnameable. This stimulation is beyond the subject on either side of the cut. It is poignancy itself. A great cut brings forth the eerie, poetic order of things.

The second aftershock is based on the literal implications of the sequence of images. It activates the logic and thought processes that are our daytime mind. Sometimes we call it meaning. It is the simple narrative sense we have for survival.

The three elements of the hierarchy have to be well-proportioned and in the proper order for a film to echo accurately the fullness of our being. First, the cut has to work spatially, then the poetic connectives must resonate, and finally there must be some sense of the meaningful or inevitable. The climactic scene of *The Passion of Joan of Arc* is a perfect example of this hierarchy. We see a flock of birds circling high in the sky intercut with burning logs and close ups of Joan at the stake, inhaling the rising smoke. The cuts between the birds and Joan have a visual vitality but also the poetic resonance of soaring and release in contrast with her suffering. A moment later, our mind turns to the thought of heaven, to the logic of the story.

When the hierarchy is out of order or one element is out of proportion, the cuts lose their vibrancy. The aliveness of the cinematic space collapses. For instance, if a cut sacrifices the spatial or the poetic in order to establish literal meaning, then there's a conceptual closure, there's no adventure, and the audience has less room to participate in the experience. This closure brings a substitute reality to the screen. The weakness of the overly symbolic moment from *La Notte* can be explained in terms of this imbalance. The selection of shots and cuts from that scene are there only to symbolize meaning. Visual grace and the potential for discovery through open-ended evocation are abandoned.

Another imbalance can arise when a cut, although visually strong, has no poignancy, or makes no sense whatsoever, or the sense it does make is dully descriptive or banal. Music-video-type editing is an obvious example of this imbalance. A film can also be falsely poetic. It may have an unusual or sophisticated visual allure but the shots and cuts ignore the delicate and mysterious necessities of meaning and therefore true visual articulation is not achieved. The entire visual effect is deadened by a lack, or an excess, of meaning. This imbalance is not uncommon in the avant-garde.

When the cuts do respect the hierarchy, the shots are permitted to breathe and are enlivened. At the same time, the cuts themselves refresh the space with clarity. When all this is functioning and wedded to its subject matter, a film becomes like a leopard walking across a room—beautiful, liquid, and full of meaning.

The films of John Ford can be noble examples of this. His shots peer *into* the oncoming light. We, the audience, the camera, are in darkness, gazing into the ephemeral, luminous world. The concreteness of heaven and earth, and the verticality of the human spine, are Ford's cosmic architecture. The cuts are crystalline synapses of confidence igniting the cinematic air. The story is expressed by the progression of shots and cuts themselves.

Ozu's highly disciplined but selfless view is deepened by cuts that are subtle jolts or shifts in space, little awakenings that underline the transparency of the moment. Each shot, enhanced by a clear and declarative cut, is transformed into a package of space with its own precise weight. The screen, in union with its subject matter, becomes a luminous square—a reflecting pool of surface tension and depth. Within this delicate structure the characters have the freedom to be. *Late Spring*

(1949), so continually ripe with this state of cinematic revelation, ends with a final cut to the open ocean. All the suffering of the human circumstances we have so tenderly experienced throughout the narrative are suddenly dissolved into a transparent, elusive memory, just as life itself, at the moment of death, may fall from our minds like nighttime dreams disappearing into our morning activities.

And who can forget Jean-Luc Godard's cut in *Contempt* (1963) from the auto accident of the red sports car to the glistening blue sea as Michel Piccoli ascends the cliffs? So much emptiness, so much spirit, so much narrative purpose is encapsulated by that cut. Which brings to mind the last cut in *Voyage to Italy*. From the climactic catharsis of the embracing Ingrid Bergman and George Sanders we cut to a seemingly insignificant detail, a uniformed town official standing amid the passing crowd. The emptiness of this strange and poignant shot is completely disarming.

The film, however, does not end there. Renzo Rossellini's music, which had been accompanying this mysterious last image, then continues as we cut to black, and the music plays on in darkness. All the poignancy and ambiguity of the love affair that we have so fully experienced now moves beyond the surface of the screen and into the very room in which we are seated.

These films are successful not only because of

their intelligence and nobility but because their expression comes from the material of cinema itself, the cinematic qualities that are deeply akin to our own metabolism. All is present, all is considered, all is working moment to moment. Like our hands, the trees, the drama of the seasons, and the warming and expiring heavens, the basic elements of film must partake in the beauty of the deepest practicality.

Devotion is not an idea or a sentiment. It is born out of the vastness and depth of our view. Out of darkness, behind all light, this vastness abides in nowness. It reveals our world. It is humbling and accurate and yet, for all its pervasiveness, it is not solid.

That the ineffable quality of vision can be expressed by projected light within darkness gives film great power. When a film is fully manifest it may serve as a mirror that realigns our psyches and opens us to appreciation and humility. The more film expresses itself in a manner intrinsic to its own true nature, the more it can reveal for us. Similarly, the more we are open to ourselves and are willing to touch the depths of our own being, the more we are participating in devotion.

Afterword

I would like to thank P. Adams Sitney and Jeffrey Stout of Princeton University for inviting me to speak at the Conference on Religion and Cinema that they convened in March, 2001. I wish also to thank Mary Lea Bandy and Antonio Monda for encouraging me to offer this essay for inclusion in their book, *The Hidden God: Film and Faith*. Their interest and enthusiasm encouraged me to refine the original talk for the written page.

I am also indebted to Konrad Steiner and Nancy Kates, who so generously transcribed my earlier lectures at the University of California, Berkeley and at Stanford University, and to Freude Bartlett and Gail Evenari, who took an early interest in bringing them into print.

The *Devotional Cinema* manuscript was carefully read over by P. Adams Sitney, Larry Fagin, Rinchen Lhamo, and David Frankel of the Museum of Modern Art. Their editorial skill and thoroughness helped me weed out unnecessary or awkward remnants of spoken syntax. Mark Butler, Paul Glickler, Vivian Kurz, Elea Mideke, Susan Vigil, and Anne Waldman assisted with more general observations. Veronica Selver helped me to translate the final lines of Georges Bernanos's *Diary of a Country Priest* from the original French;

those lines now stand as the epigraph to this book.

I want to acknowledge again the kindness of Nick Hoff in helping me refine this text and to express my enormous gratitude to him; without his intelligent, inquiring editorial companionship this would be a far lesser book.

And finally, my thanks go to Owsley Brown III, whose inspiration and generosity have made the Tuumba Press editions of *Devotional Cinema* possible.

This third, revised edition of
Devotional Cinema
was printed in an edition of 2000 copies
at McNaughton & Gunn.
Original design is by Travis Ortiz;
original typesetting is by
Claire Marie Stancek
using Adobe's version
of the classic typeface Garamond.
Additions to the revised edition
are by Derek Fenner.
The cover design is by Ree Katrak /
Great Bay Graphics.